CONSERVATION CHAMPIONS!

REUSING AND RECYCLING WASTE

SADIE SILVA

Enslow PUBLISHING

Please visit our website, www.enslow.com.
For a free color catalog of all our high-quality books, call toll free 1-800-398-2504 or fax 1-877-980-4454.

Library of Congress Cataloging-in-Publication Data
Names: Silva, Sadie author
Title: Reusing and recycling waste / Sadie Silva.
Description: Buffalo, NY : Enslow Publishing, [2027] | Series: Conservation champions! | Includes index.
Identifiers: LCCN 2025055136 (print) | LCCN 2025055137 (ebook) | ISBN 9781978547803 library binding | ISBN 9781978547797 paperback | ISBN 9781978547810 ebook
Subjects: LCSH: Recycling (Waste, etc.) | Refuse and refuse disposal | Environmental protection–Citizen participation | Housekeeping–Environmental aspects | Handicraft
Classification: LCC TD794.5 .S55 2027 (print) | LCC TD794.5 (ebook) | DDC 363.72/82–dc23/eng/20260309
LC record available at https://lccn.loc.gov/2025055136
LC ebook record available at https://lccn.loc.gov/2025055137

Published in 2027 by
Enslow Publishing
2544 Clinton Street
Buffalo, NY 14224

Designer: Tanya Dellaccio Keeney
Editor: Therese Shea

Photo credits: Cover (boy) Veja/Shutterstock.com; cover (clothes) Pixel-Shot/Shutterstock.com; p. 5 BOY ANTHONY/Shutterstock.com; p. 7 (landfill) Jenya Smyk/Shutterstock.com; p. 7 (ocean) Andrewfel/Shutterstock.com; p. 9 SYB_16/Shutterstock.com; p. 11 (beads) Lea Rae/Shutterstock.com; p. 11 (woman with bag) Andrey Zhorov/Shutterstock.com; p. 13 Maryana Volkova/Shutterstock.com; p. 15 VanderWolf Images/Shutterstock.com; p. 17 Gorodenkoff/Shutterstock.com; p. 19 New Africa/Shutterstock.com; p. 21 Julia Kostiuchenko/Shutterstock.com.

Printed in the United States of America

CPSIA compliance information: Batch #CSENS27: For further information contact Enslow Publishing, at 1-800-398-2504.

CONTENTS

BOLDFACE WORDS APPEAR IN THE GLOSSARY.

THE THREE Rs

Have you heard of the three Rs? They stand for reduce, reuse, and recycle. These are three ways people can cut down on waste. Reducing means using less. Reusing means using something more than once. Recycling means changing waste into something usable.

IN THIS BOOK, YOU'LL LEARN MORE ABOUT REUSING AND RECYCLING.

WHY NOT WASTE?

Making too much waste is harmful. It sends more trash to **landfills**. Landfills cause **pollution**. As trash breaks down in landfills, it may give off harmful gases. It may break down into harmful **chemicals** that get into water and soil. Some plastic trash takes hundreds of years to break down.

MUCH TRASH DOESN'T EVEN MAKE IT TO LANDFILLS. IT ENDS UP IN NATURE, INCLUDING OUR OCEANS.

LANDFILL

Reusing and recycling save **natural resources** such as metals, trees, and water. That's because fewer metals are mined and fewer trees are cut down to make new products. Producing new goods also requires power, such as **electricity**, and water.

MINING METALS RUINS LAND FOR PLANTS AND ANIMALS. CUTTING DOWN TREES DOES TOO.

COAL MINE

REUSE IT

What kinds of things can you reuse? Your food from the store might come in plastic boxes or glass jars. You can reuse some of these containers after you clean them. Plastic and paper bags can be reused too.

PEOPLE OFTEN TAKE REUSABLE BAGS TO THE STORE. THIS CUTS DOWN ON THE AMOUNT OF PLASTIC OR PAPER BAGS USED AND THROWN AWAY.

THAT'S CREATIVE

You can reuse some objects for their **original** purpose, such as storing food. You can use them for a new purpose too. For example, cardboard boxes can be made into forts. A plastic container can hold art supplies. Clothing can be reused too. Pants can be made into shorts, for example.

CLOTHING WASTE IS A BIG PROBLEM. **DAMAGED** OR OLD CLOTHING CAN BE FIXED OR MADE INTO OTHER ITEMS!

RECYCLE IT

If you can't reuse something, you might be able to recycle it. Some plastics can be recycled. So can glass, paper, and metal objects. At a recycling plant, these things are sorted. They're crushed into big blocks. Then, they're sent to factories where they're made into new products.

THIS PHOTO SHOWS BLOCKS OF PLASTIC AT A RECYCLING PLANT.

Cities and towns have rules about what can be recycled. Find out what you can and can't recycle. Some communities have times when special things can be recycled, such as **electronics** and **batteries**. These things shouldn't go into landfills.

COMPUTERS AND OTHER ELECTRONICS HAVE VALUABLE METALS IN THEM THAT CAN BE REUSED OR RECYCLED.

BE A CHAMPION!

A champion is someone who fights for a cause. You can be a champion for Earth! Reusing and recycling are two ways to fight pollution and other harm that comes from too much waste. The more you recycle and reuse, the easier it becomes.

REUSING AND RECYCLING TAKES SOME THOUGHT. THINK BEFORE YOU THROW OUT!

ACTIVITY

- Tell an adult in your home why you'd like to reuse and recycle more.
- Create a poster to put above your trash can. On it, ask others to think about reusing or recycling before throwing something out.
- Put two bins next to the trash can.
- One is for reusing, and one is for recycling. Label each.
- After a day, check the bins. Ask an adult if you're unsure about how something can be reused or recycled.

GLOSSARY

battery: A device that turns chemical energy into electricity.

chemical: Matter that can be mixed with other matter to cause changes.

damaged: Harmed or spoiled.

electricity: The flow of electrical energy.

electronics: Parts, tools, and machinery that use electricity.

landfill: A place where garbage is buried.

natural resource: Something in nature that can be used by people.

original: First or earliest.

pollution: The act of making land, water, or air unsafe for people or animals.

FOR MORE INFORMATION

BOOKS

Greenfield, Rob. *Zero Waste Kids: Hands-on Projects and Activities to Reduce, Reuse, and Recycle*. Beverly, MA: Quarry Books, 2022.

Redshaw, Hermione. *Making a Difference from Home*. Minneapolis, MN: Bearport Publishing, 2023.

WEBSITES

A Kid-Friendly Guide to Recycling

kids.earth.org/life-on-land/a-kid-friendly-guide-to-recycling/
Read more tips about recycling the right way.

13 Ways to Save the Earth from Pollution

kids.nationalgeographic.com/nature/save-the-earth/article/13-ways-to-save-the-earth-from-pollution
Discover more ways to be a conservation champion!

INDEX